Tell Me Why
Love, Sex & Babies

BY ARKADY LEOKUM

Illustrations by Richard Powers

HAMLYN
LONDON · NEW YORK · SYDNEY · TORONTO

FOREWORD

This is a book that is honest. It does not pretend to be a definitive sex education book. There cannot be such a book, for individual attitudes to the complex matters of sex education, general education, child care and, of course, politics, are so varied. (And never think political attitudes don't come into the matter of sex education; they definitely do. There are conservative methods of teaching children about sex, liberal and radical ones, even anarchic ones.)

There has for a long time been a fashion for sex education writers to tell parents to be "free", "open-ended", and "relaxed" in dealing with their children's questions about sex, which is excellent advice for people with free, open-ended, relaxed personalities. But there are plenty of people who are not like this. They have a rather more organised approach to life, preferring to have their lines clearly delineated, liking to structure their attitudes along well defined pathways, enjoying being part of an hierarchical society rather than strongly individualistic. The fact that these are traditional attitudes does not automatically mean they are fuddy-duddy – and it is a pity that so many moderns use the word "traditional" as a sneer. Not all the old values are outworn; and anyway in a free society there is room for many different opinions.

And that is why this book has a place amid the many others that have been produced for parents facing the question "What shall we tell the children?" It spells out clear answers to a great many questions children ask about love, sex and babies, in a way that is simple and direct. Parents who find themselves blushing and tongue-tied when asked to talk about sex should not add guilt to the burden of their shyness; they are as they are, and trying to go against their essential natures will only create disagreeable internal upheaval – and that is hardly helpful to parent or child. Instead, they should put this book into their children's hands and let them seek their own information from it. They can be assured that their children will not be given ideas that differ radically from their own, but that they will emerge from their reading with a number of useful facts. If, later on, these same children choose to be less traditional than their parents, then the facts and ideas they have found in this book will not be an embarrassment to them. They will form an excellent jumping-off point for further fact-and-idea searching. And one can ask little more of a children's book than that.

Claire Rayner

Published in 1975
by The Hamlyn Publishing Group Limited
Astronaut House, Hounslow Road, Feltham, Middlesex, England
© Copyright 1974 by Arkady Leokum
All rights reserved under International and Pan-American Copyright Conventions
Published pursuant to agreement with
Grosset and Dunlap Inc., New York, N.Y., U.S.A.
ISBN 0 600 38715 1
Printed in Czechoslovakia by PZ, Bratislava
51123/1

CONTENTS

BABIES

Love

Love

WHAT IS LOVE?

There is no simple way to explain, or define, "love". It is a strong emotional involvement with another person. It shows itself by the way we keep thinking of them and wanting to be with them, by the way we want them to be happy and to do things for them. It may be, for some, the strongest emotion they will ever feel.

The word "love" can be used to express such emotional feelings as "I love my country" or "I love my dog". These can be very strongly felt emotions, but the love between a man and a woman is deeper and more personal and has more meaning.

AT WHAT AGE DO PEOPLE FALL IN LOVE?

There is no specific age when this happens, but a person must be mature in certain ways to experience love. Young people do feel strong attachments for each other, and imagine at times they are "in love". But the full, deep meaning of loving another person can only be understood when one is mature. There is a responsibility that comes with love, and a dedication of oneself to the person one love that very young people cannot feel.

IS A MOTHER'S LOVE FOR HER CHILDREN THE SAME AS HER LOVE FOR HER HUSBAND?

No. And it should not be. It is not a question of "less love" or "more love", it is simply a different kind of love. A mother can love a child "with all her heart", and this will mean being devoted to the child, caring for it, helping it in every way, being close and warm and understanding, and making sacrifices for the child. But it is different from her love for her husband.

That love – for her husband – involves her in a different way. It shows itself, among other things, in wanting to be physically close to him, in making love (having sexual intercourse). It reaches a beautiful closeness that is just as precious as her closeness to her children – and it does not conflict with her love for her children.

WHY DO SOME PEOPLE HAVE MANY CLOSE RELATIONSHIPS WITH MEMBERS OF THE OPPOSITE SEX BEFORE THEY GET MARRIED?

It is possible to be emotionally involved with another person only up to a point. The relationship may not be strong or deep enough for the two people to want to marry each other.

Also, as a person becomes older and more mature, one's taste may change, or one's interests, or what one wants out of life. This can lead to people growing apart from each other. One may even become disappointed in some way with a person and discover that he or she was not the right person to make one happy.

IS IT POSSIBLE TO LOVE A FRIEND?

Of course. But it will be a different feeling with a dear friend. Having a good time together, enjoying each other's company, admiring a friend, even feeling completely devoted to a friend, all this is a kind of "love". At the same time, one can feel a strong emotional attachment to another person. Each feeling has its place in our lives.

CAN A MAN AND A WOMAN LOVE EACH OTHER WITHOUT WANTING SEX?

It is possible, and it has happened to many people. But the feeling of love between a man and a woman reaches its deepest level when they can be close in the act of love.

Sex becomes an expression and a fulfilment of their love for each other, so it is usual for them to want to experience this.

DO PARENTS LOVE ALL THEIR CHILDREN EQUALLY?

"Equally" does not necessarily mean in the same way. A mother may feel a deep love for her son and show it in a different way than she does her love for her daughter. Sometimes children in a family are so different from each other, with different personalities and needs, that parents express their love for them quite differently.

And sometimes there is a "favourite" child, perhaps the only son among several girls, or the only daughter among several sons, or a child with some special weakness who needs special love, or a child having some talent that the parents try to develop. The other children may resist it, or be jealous. Unfortunately, this situation does exist in some families.

DO PEOPLE EVER GET MARRIED WITHOUT BEING IN LOVE?

Yes. Nobody wants to, but sometimes it does arise. In certain families and societies, marriages are arranged by the parents – for financial or other reasons.

Sometimes people reach a certain age unmarried and feel so lonely that they get married for the sake of sharing life with another person. Such a marriage can develop so that the two people feel great affection for each other.

CAN A MAN OR A WOMAN LOVE TWO DIFFERENT PEOPLE AT THE SAME TIME?

Some men and women feel they can. You have probably seem films or read books in which a man loves two different women or vice versa. Does the man love both women in the same way? If the women are quite unlike each other, he may love them for their different qualities. This is equally true for a woman loving two men.

14

But most people believe that the love between a man and a woman makes it impossible for them to share that feeling with other people.

CAN PEOPLE OF DIFFERENT RACES FALL IN LOVE?

Yes, and often do. They have been doing it for thousands of years all over the world.

But society has not made it easy for such people. Laws have even been passed in certain places forbidding relationships or marriages between people of different races, in some cases because of prejudice, or ignorance about the other race, or a feeling that it is harmful to "mix" races.

Many people today feel it is perfectly natural and acceptable for men and women of different races to love each other and marry.

DO MEN EVER LOVE MEN, AND
WOMEN LOVE WOMEN?

There is a feeling that men can have for men, and women have for women, that is the love friends feel for each other. It can be very strong and last a lifetime.

But if there is a sexual attraction, it is called "homosexual" love. This kind of love does take place, and is considered true love by the people involved.

WHY DO PEOPLE SOMETIMES FALL
OUT OF LOVE?

There is no single or simple explanation. It is sad when it happens, and seems to be something beyond "control". A person may simply begin to feel that he or she is no longer happy in the relationship. This can be brought about by two people growing away from each other and developing apart so that they lose the ability to share each other's interests.

AS MARRIED PEOPLE GET OLDER, DO THEY LOVE EACH OTHER LESS?

If two people have shared a loving relationship through the years, they will continue to do so as they approach old age. But the expression and quality of that love may change with age. Instead of passion, there may be tenderness. Instead of a desire to kiss, hug, and make love, there may be only the need and desire to be together, keep each other company, take care of each other. This stage of love can be just as important and beautiful to older people as their young love was.

DO THE CHILDREN IN A FAMILY ALWAYS LOVE EACH OTHER?

Unfortunately, no. It often happens that there is jealousy, or basic differences in character, temperament or interests that set children in a family against each other. It has happened in many families for thousands of years.

But usually, even if they do not all "love" each other, the children in a family still feel the close ties and are concerned for each other.

CAN A BROTHER AND SISTER FALL IN LOVE?

Yes. It is very rare, because religion and our society do not approve of it. So, as brothers and sisters grow up together, they are trained and encouraged to grow fond of members of the opposite sex outside the family. A brother and a sister can feel very close and have great affection for each other, and feel nothing beyond that – and be very happy about their relationship.

CAN A CHILD HATE HIS FATHER OR MOTHER?

At an early age, many children say, "I hate you, Daddy!" or, "I hate you, Mummy!" And they feel they really do. This may be because of enforced discipline, or because of attitudes or opinions the parents have, or because certain things the children feel they want are being denied them.

As these children grow older, they realise that they did not really "hate" their father or mother, and they may forget they ever felt that way.

But there are cases where a child really does hate his parent or parents. There may be many reasons for this, but it is a sign that "something went wrong" in the relationship. Sometimes the parents are to blame. Their lack of understanding of the child, or the way they treated the child, may be responsible. In other cases, the child may be wrong in his own attitudes and feelings, bringing about "hate".

Whatever the reason, such things do happen and cause much unhappiness to children and parents.

CAN ONE LOVE ANOTHER PERSON MORE THAN ONE'S OWN PARENTS?

The love one has for a parent can never be replaced, because the relationship can never be replaced by anyone else.

18

But a person can feel a love for someone else that is different, and sometimes it can be stronger. It is usually the love for a person one wants to marry and live with and have a family.

It is normal and right for this kind of love to be so overwhelming that one is ready to leave one's parents, perhaps even move far away sometimes and not see them for long periods.

Most parents accept this and expect it. After all, they may have done it themselves to *their* parents.

DO PEOPLE HAVE TO BE ABOUT THE SAME AGE TO FALL IN LOVE?

No. But it is usually the case, because people of the same age go out together, do things together, and have the same interests and goals in life. And if they are about the same age, it is natural for them to be physically attracted to each other.

Many older people of approximately the same age who happen to be divorced, widowed, or living alone, will fall in love for the same reasons – they are attracted to one another and can enjoy the life they want together.

WHY DO WE SOMETIMES FEEL THAT NOBODY LOVES US?

Because sometimes nobody does – at least, in the way we want to be loved. We all want other people, friends and parents, to think of us, remember us, do things for us. Sometimes these "other people" do not do it exactly when – and in the way – we would like. They may have their own problems and disappointments, or be busy, or simply forget.

But very often these same people – our parents and friends – later *do* come through and show they love us.

DO YOUR PARENTS HAVE TO LIKE THE PERSON YOU FALL IN LOVE WITH?

You *hope* they do because it would give you and the person you love a feeling of approval and acceptance within your family.

But in some cases this not happen. Some young people today are not even asking their parents' approval of the person they are going to marry. So there is no "must" about it. It varies from family to family, depending upon the relationship. But it *is* nice when it happens.

IF WE "LOVE" A PET, LIKE A DOG OR A HORSE, IS THAT REALLY LOVE?

It is a natural, wonderful, even exciting kind of love one can have for a pet – but it is not the same kind of love one can feel for another person. The great thing about it is that one can feel both kinds of love at the same time, enjoy them both, and still know which is really the more important and more meaningful.

ARE THERE SOME PEOPLE WHO NEVER GET MARRIED?

Yes. It does not mean they cannot, or do not want to. They may not have fallen in love and decided to marry because they have never met the right person for them. Or it sometimes happens that certain people are "afraid" to marry, because it would mean changing their way of life, assuming responsibilities, sharing their home and possessions with someone else. Such people may love their parents, or brothers and sisters, but never be able to give themselves to another person in marriage.

CAN PRIESTS, MINISTERS, AND RABBIS FALL IN LOVE?

Ministers of certain religions, and rabbis of the Jewish faith, are permitted to marry – so they do allow themselves to fall in love.

Priests of the Catholic faith are not permitted to marry, so they avoid "falling in love". They feel their love of God and of their fellow men is a greater kind of love. But there have been cases where priests have fallen in love and married, and have left the priesthood as a result.

WHY ARE THERE SO MANY BOOKS, FILMS AND SONGS ABOUT LOVE?

Love is one of the strongest and most beautiful experiences anyone can have. It affects some people so strongly and deeply that they want to express what they feel and pay tribute to this great emotion. So they write songs, poems, plays, and books about it.

And since everyone is curious about love, or has felt it, or hopes to feel it, there is always a receptive, appreciative audience for such songs, books and films.

WHAT DOES IT MEAN TO "LOVE YOUR FELLOW MAN"?

It means one should be concerned with other people, with their happiness, security, and progress. It means one should care what happens to other people, even if they are strangers, or quite different from ourselves. It means one should be willing to help them, even at some sacrifice to ourselves. Love for our fellow man is one of the basic principles of all great religions of the world.

DO ANIMALS FALL IN LOVE?

"Falling in love" among human beings involves not just sexual attraction, but also a mental and emotional involvement. Our whole person feels something for another individual's whole person.

But animals have a more limited attraction for each other. It is a sexual attraction that involves courtship and mating, but it takes place because of an instinct, the instinct to reproduce the species.

Sounds that are created, such as songs, colours that are displayed, such as in feathers of birds, certain "dances" that are done by animals and insects – all of these attract animals to each other.

WHAT DOES THE HEART HAVE TO
DO WITH LOVE?

Nothing, really. The heart is like a pump in our body whose job it is to circulate our blood. And even though people will say, "I love you with all my heart", it is not in the heart that we feel all the things we do when we are in love. Still, the heart has become a symbol of love.

Why did this happen? Probably because when we do feel a very strong emotion, the action of our heart is affected. When we are excited, the heart beats more rapidly. When we are frightened, our heart seems to "stand still". When we are upset or sad, our heartbeat slows up. So, since the heart reacts to what we are feeling, we have come to think of the heart as being the seat of love.

WHY ARE PEOPLE IN LOVE
OFTEN JEALOUS?

When we love somebody, we feel we are giving "all of ourselves" to that person. We like to think that the person we love feels the same way about us. And when we think this is not happening – when the person we love displays such feelings for someone else, too – we tend to become jealous. We are apprehensive that this other person will take our place. A bit of jealousy is a rather natural feeling to have, but when carried too far, it can create problems between people.

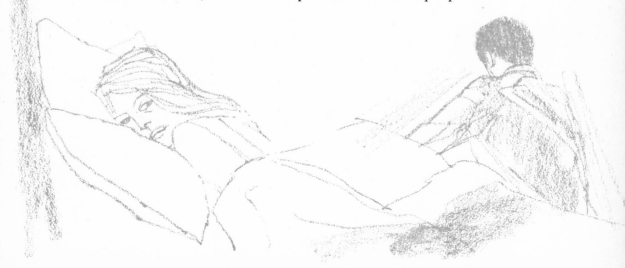

WHY DO PEOPLE GO ON HONEYMOONS?

In very ancient times, a bridegroom had to "capture" his bride. He would then have to hide somewhere with her until her relatives or tribespeople grew tired of searching for her. It is believed that the honeymoon developed as a symbol of what took place in those days.

So, to some extent, people still go on honeymoons because it is the traditional thing to do, just as they do many other "symbolic" things connected with marriage.

But newly married people enjoy going on a honeymoon because it gives them a chance to get to know each other intimately, and relate to each other. It is ideally spent in a place and atmosphere far from the bothers or problems of workaday life.

WHY DO PEOPLE GET DIVORCED?

There is no single reason for divorce; there are many. Quite simply, it is because one of the partners, or both, decide that the marriage should end. The reason could be because they cannot get along together anymore, or one of them has fallen in love with someone else, or done something that has destroyed the marriage.

CAN'T PEOPLE WHO LOVE EACH OTHER LIVE TOGETHER WITHOUT GETTING MARRIED?

Of course they can, and many people have done it. Some young people today feel that it is not "necessary" ever to get married formally.

There is no law that forces a man and woman who live together to be married – though members of certain religions are condemned by that religion if they do not.

But the society in which we live, including many of its laws and customs, is built around the idea of marriage. Wives have certain rights and protection that marriage gives them. Children of a legal marriage are entitled to certain things under law. And most people we meet believe in marriage and have strong attitudes about it.

So a couple that decides not to get married must be prepared to give up certain benefits, and face certain problems for themselves and their children. But they do have the right to make that choice.

WHAT IS BIGAMY?

When a man is married to more than one wife, or a woman to more than one husband, it is called bigamy. It is considered a crime in most countries of the western world.

The way it usually happens is that a marriage is still in force, and one of the partners gets married again without ending the first marriage legally.

IS SEXUAL INTERCOURSE
PART OF MARRIAGE?

Animals have an instinct that attracts them to each other so they can mate and reproduce. Nature has provided human beings with an attraction for each other, too, so they can reproduce.

This attraction among human beings, which we call love, is expressed in many ways. It is a devotion, a concern for the other person, a desire to give them happiness, and a desire to live together with them. That is why people get married.

The fulfillment of the marriage takes place in many ways, too. It is a sharing together, a joining of feelings, a union. The expression of that union comes about through sexual intercourse. It does not take the place of other things in their life together, spiritual and mental, which are important. But it is part of the need they feel, and part of the joy they have in a complete and happy marriage.

Sex

Sex

WHAT IS A VIRGIN?

A virgin is a person who has never had sexual intercourse.

Some people believe a virgin is a female whose hymen has not been broken. The hymen is a membrane (layer of tissues) that partly closes the entrance to the vagina, but in some females an opening in the hymen develops without sexual intercourse, and there are even cases where a female has no hymen at all.

HOW OFTEN DO MARRIED PEOPLE HAVE SEX?

It varies with each couple. There is no such thing as a "normal" number of times per week or month. It could be anywhere from several times a day to once a year.

It does seem, on the average, to have something to do with the age of the couple. There are studies which show that under the age of 25 married couples have intercourse about 7 times a month, at ages 35 to 44 about 4 times a month, and after the age of 55 about once a month.

AT WHAT AGE ARE BOYS ABLE TO HAVE SEXUAL INTERCOURSE?

For a male, having sexual intercourse means to ejaculate (throw out suddenly) semen from his penis into the vagina of a female.

Boys are able to do this when they reach the age of puberty, which is usually when they are about 13 or 14 years old. But some boys reach puberty as early as the age of 10 or 11, and others do not until they are about 15.

WHAT IS PUBERTY?

We say a young person has reached puberty when certain changes begin to take place in the body.

In a boy, hair (called "pubic hair") begins to grow in the genital area above the penis. Hair also starts to grow under the arms. The penis becomes larger. The voice becomes deeper. He begins to grow taller. All of these changes take place over a period of about two years.

In a girl, her breasts begin to develop. She also grows pubic hair. Her figure becomes larger and she may gain weight. Puberty can begin in a girl at the age of 11, but the average age is about 13 years.

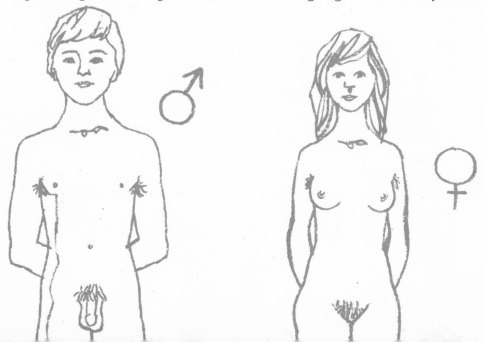

AT WHAT AGE CAN A BOY BECOME A FATHER?

When he has reached puberty, because his body now creates sperm cells. And since different boys reach that stage at different times (the average age is about 14), this can even happen at the age of 11 or 12, in some cases.

AT WHAT AGE IS A GIRL ABLE TO HAVE SEXUAL INTERCOURSE?

When she begins to menstruate – because now her body produces ova, eggs that can be fertilised by sperm cells. Menstruation usually starts between 12 and 14 years of age.

WHY DON'T GIRLS HAVE A PENIS?

The sex organs of the male and the female are made so that they function together. They are like lock and key. The key fits into the lock.

The male has a penis so that in sexual intercourse it is capable of depositing sperm in the female's vagina. The female has a vagina so that it can receive the penis and the sperm.

WHAT IS MASTURBATION?

Masturbation is handling one's sex organs to produce excitement and pleasure.

Males usually do it by holding the penis with the closed hand and moving the hand back and forth until there is an ejaculation . . . an orgasm.

Females usually do it by rubbing the hand or a finger over the clitoris, which is a very small organ above the entrance to the vagina. The clitoris becomes erect when it is stimulated and the female has an orgasm.

DO ALL BOYS AND GIRLS MASTURBATE?

People who have made studies of this subject say that by the age of 15 practically all boys have masturbated. In other words, nearly 100 per cent masturbate.

With girls, the figure is lower. By the age of 15, about 25 per cent of the girls have masturbated. But surveys also indicate that by the time females have become mature, about 60 per cent of them have masturbated.

IS IT HARMFUL TO THE BODY OR THE MIND TO MASTURBATE?

No, there is no harm in masturbation. In fact, it relieves sexual tension in the body. It is certainly not true that masturbation can affect a person's mind, or do harm to the body causing pimples to appear or bringing dark circles under the eyes. Masturbation when young does not create problems in sexual adjustment when one is adult.

CAN IT BE WRONG TO MASTURBATE?

Yes. Some religions condemn it, so it may make a person who is religious feel guilty if he or she does it. Such feelings of guilt would make it wrong to masturbate.

Certain groups in society, or parents, can cause a young person to feel this way, too. If masturbating brings on a strong sense of guilt – enough to really cause unhappiness – it should be avoided.

As a person grows older and forms relationships, other sexual outlets are possible. But if masturbation still remains a person's only sexual outlet, it is not good.

WHY DO PEOPLE MASTURBATE?

The desire for sexual pleasure and release appears in people naturally. Human beings discovered, thousands and thousands of years ago, that masturbating is a way of obtaining this pleasure and release when other ways are not possible. It can be done alone, it harms no one, it is not dangerous to health, and it provides the relief from a kind of tension that sexual need builds up in us.

Sometimes, however, boys and girls masturbate for other reasons, as for example, when they feel lonely, or are upset by relationships with their parents or friends, or even when they have problems at school. They resort to masturbation as a means of making themselves feel better.

When these are the reasons for masturbating, it is better to try to work out the problems in more practical ways, such as getting advice or help.

IS IT WRONG TO HAVE SEX WITHOUT WANTING TO PRODUCE A BABY?

No. Sex between people who love each other is a way of expressing that love. Husbands and wives want to have sexual intercourse because of what they feel for each other. That is normal and healthy, and it can be beautiful. So couples do not have to limit intercourse only to times when they want to produce a baby.

WHAT IS AN ERECTION?

An erection is a hardening of the penis so that it becomes firm, becomes longer, and stands up and away from the body. In this way it becomes ready for sexual intercourse.

What enables this to happen is that the male is sexually stimulated in some way – in his mind or by physical contact. This "stimulus" goes to the nervous system which reacts by causing a flow of blood from the arteries into the penis.

Within the penis, blood vessels and cavities that are part of certain "erectile" tissues become so filled with blood that the penis becomes firm and erect.

WHAT IS THE HYMEN?

The hymen is a layer of tissue (called a membrane) which surrounds the outer opening of the vagina. Usually, the first time a female has sexual intercourse, the hymen is ruptured or broken, but sometimes it stretches and does not tear. So whether the hymen is broken or not is not a sure sign of whether the female is a "virgin".

WHAT IS THE UTERUS?

The uterus is the same as the "womb", an organ in the female behind the vagina about the size of a small fist. When an egg has been fertilised by a sperm cell, it comes down into the uterus from what is called the Fallopian tube.

The uterus nourishes and protects the fertilised egg until it becomes a baby ready to be born. Then the muscular walls of the uterus act to bring the baby out of the body. The walls of the uterus are elastic, so they stretch out during pregnancy and then return to their original thickness after the baby is born.

WHAT IS THE VAGINA?

The vagina is the passage leading to the uterus. The penis is placed in vagina during sexual intercourse and deposits the sperm cells.

The vagina is made up of very elastic muscular tissue, which is why a baby can pass through it during childbirth without tearing it.

From the lining of the vagina comes an acid fluid which serves to keep it clean and to lubricate it. In an adult female, the vagina is about 3 inches long.

EXACTLY WHAT HAPPENS DURING SEXUAL INTERCOURSE?

Basically, sexual intercourse takes place when the male penis enters the female vagina and releases sperm cells there.

But there is a great deal more that happens, emotionally and physically. Both the male and the female are first stimulated – that is, their desire to have sexual intercourse is aroused. It can come about through kissing and caressing each other. Each couple has its own way of doing this to express their love or desire.

In the male, erection takes place. His penis becomes firm and hard. In the female, changes take place, too. The vulva, which is at the opening of the vagina, swells a little. The clitoris, which is a small, buttonlike organ at the very top of the vulva, also becomes erect. The vagina becomes relaxed so the penis can enter it, and it becomes moistened inside. The nipples on the breast become erect.

All of these things are taking place before the male inserts his penis. Now the male and female are ready for intercourse.

The female usually lies on her back and spreads her legs apart and draws up her knees. The male, lying on top of her, inserts his penis into her vagina. He then moves his penis back and forth, and the female also moves back and forth with her hips.

Because of the friction of the penis against the walls of the vagina, the male ejaculates – has an orgasm – sending out sperm cells into the vagina.

Because of the feeling of the penis rubbing on the clitoris and inside the vagina, the female also has an orgasm. That is, she feels a strong sensation of pleasure that comes to a climax.

After an orgasm, both the male and the female have a sense of relaxation and a feeling of satisfaction. The male's penis becomes soft and he takes it out of the vagina.

The sexual intercourse is over, but the feeling of closeness and love for each other can be stronger than ever.

WHAT IS BIRTH CONTROL?

Birth control, or contraception, is the prevention of a sperm cell from fertilising an egg cell – preventing the creation of a baby.

There are many ways in which it may be done, and many reasons why it is done. Parents may feel they do not want any more children. Or the male and the female having sexual intercourse may not be married, and so not want a child. Such people feel that birth control is a perfectly right and moral thing to do.

But there are also people who have religious or personal reasons for thinking that birth control is a wrong thing to do.

WHY DOES THE CATHOLIC CHURCH SAY THAT BIRTH CONTROL IS WRONG?

The Catholic Church does not believe that *all* methods of birth control are wrong – only those it considers to be against the will of God, because they are not natural, such as using any devices or chemicals.

The Catholic Church approves of what is called the "rhythm method" of birth control. It means that the married couple will have intercourse during a "safe period", a time before and after ovulation occurs. Ovulation is the release of the egg (ovum) inside the female, which is generally once every 28 days. Since there is no egg to fertilise before and after ovulation, it is called the "safe period".

WHAT IS A SHEATH?

A sheath is made of extremely fine rubber shaped to fit the penis. It is put on the erect penis before intercourse takes place so that the sperm cells are prevented from entering the vagina.

WHAT IS "THE PILL"?

It is a way of practising birth control that is used by many women today. When a woman swallows this pill, chemical changes take place in her body. She does not ovulate. Since there is no egg to be fertilised, she cannot become pregnant.

But in order for it to work, a pill cannot be taken just for one day. It is taken, once a day, for 20 days, then stopped for about a week so the female can menstruate. Then it is taken again for 20 days.

A doctor's prescription is needed to obtain "the pill".

WHAT ARE THE TESTICLES?

The testicles are where the male produces the sperm cells. Every male has two of them. They are oval-shaped and in a grown man about one and a half inches long. They are located below the penis in a pouch of skin called the scrotum.

In addition to producing sperm cells, the testicles also produce male sex hormones, which go into the bloodstream. These hormones provide masculine characteristics – hair, figure, and so on.

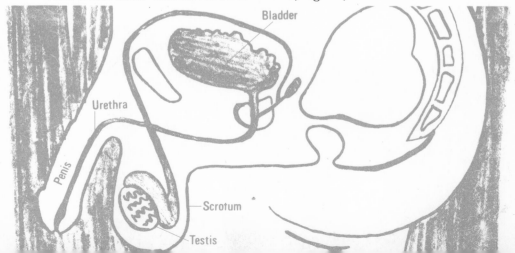

Bladder

Urethra

Penis

Scrotum

Testis

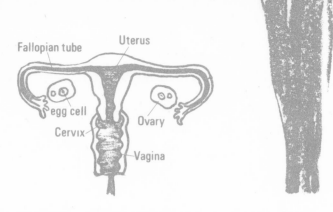

Fallopian tube — Uterus — egg cell — Cervix — Ovary — Vagina

WHAT ARE THE FUNCTIONS OF THE OVARIES?

The ovaries are two organs located in the female on each side of the womb. They are about the size of walnuts.

The ova, or egg cells and the hormones which regulate the female secondary sex characteristics develop in the ovaries. The hormones regulate various functions of the body and help make the female a "female" by giving her a feminine figure, voice and hair, developing her breasts, and so on.

The ovaries regulate the reproduction system of the female because the egg cell develops in the ovary. Menstruation occurs before ovulation, to prepare the uterus for the fertilised egg cell. The ovaries regulate the time of ovulation, when the egg cell leaves the ovary and enters the Fallopian tube. It is at this time that the male sperm cell can fertilise the female egg cell.

DO MEN WANT SEX MORE THAN WOMEN DO?

Because in our society men are expected to be the aggressors – that is, they are supposed to pursue the women and "make the advances" – it is believed that males have a greater desire for sex than females.

But in terms of biology, this is not so. The female is so built that her body can enjoy intercourse even more than a male. She can enjoy it for a longer time and experience a greater number of orgasms.

WHAT DOES IT MEAN TO BE "IMPOTENT"?

When a male's penis cannot become erect, he is considered "impotent". Or sometimes, a male does have an erection, but cannot ejaculate (give off the sperm cells).

In most cases, there is an emotional reason for this, such as nervousness, or being anxious about whether it will happen or not. When the male can overcome anxiety, the impotence usually disappears.

WHY DO MEN ADMIRE A WOMAN'S BREASTS?

A woman's breasts have become a kind of symbol of the female. They are a part of the female body that a male can always see is there, no matter how she dresses. And from the days when he was a baby at his mother's breast, the male has liked to feel and touch them.

So when a male admires a female's breasts, he is expressing interest in what excites him in a sexual way.

WHAT IS SEMEN?

Semen is the fluid that is ejaculated by the penis during sexual intercourse. It contains the sperm cells. It also contains secretions from various glands which are needed so the sperm cells will be protected.

DOES THE SEMEN COME THROUGH THE SAME TUBE IN THE PENIS AS THE URINE?

Urine and semen both come out of the same tube, called the urethra, but they are fed into the penis through different tubes.

One tube is connected with the bladder, which brings urine to the penis. Another tube goes around the bladder and is connected with the testicles, which bring sperm cells to the penis.

When there is an ejaculation, a valve shuts off the urine from the penis. The semen and urine never mix.

WHAT IS AN ORGASM?

While the act of sexual intercourse involves many feelings and physical changes, it reaches its climax – or highest point – in what is called an orgasm.

Both males and females have it. In the male there is an ejaculation of semen from the penis in spurts. There is also a sensation of the heart beating faster, a flushed feeling, an intense excitement and satisfaction.

In the female, the walls of the vagina contract in a kind of rhythm, and there is also a sensation of the heart beating faster and a flushed feeling.

The orgasm is the most intense feeling of pleasure that is experienced in sexual intercourse.

DOES THERE HAVE TO BE AN ORGASM TO CREATE A BABY?

For the male, yes. The ejaculation deposits sperm cells in the vagina during intercourse. For the female, no. She can become pregnant even if she does not have an orgasm.

WHAT IS PORNOGRAPHY?

There are magazines, books, pictures, films, which show sex, but not in an educational way. They may describe acts of sex, or show them being performed, or display naked men and women.

They are considered to be "pornography" when their purpose is to excite people sexually, or satisfy strange tastes or interests in sex. People who deliberately produce pornography do it to make money, rather than to educate people about sex.

WHY DO PEOPLE TELL "DIRTY JOKES"?

Many people have suppressed feelings about sex. That is, they are interested in it, and excited by it, but hide their feelings about it. Telling a "dirty joke" (which means a joke about sex) is for them a way of expressing this interest in what is considered a "harmless" way.

Sometimes people do not realise it, but telling dirty jokes provides a kind of release for them, a way of getting something out of their system that makes them tense or anxious.

WHY DO SOME MALES HAVE BIGGER PENISES THAN OTHERS?

For the same reason that some males have larger hands or feet. It just happens to be the size of their sex organ.

A larger penis does not mean that the male is going to get more pleasure from sex, or be more interested in sex, or perform sexual intercourse better.

WHAT IS ADOLESCENCE?

Adolescence is the period in a young person's life from puberty to adulthood. It begins in girls at ages from 11 to 15, and in boys about a year later. It lasts till they are about 19 years old.

During the first period of adolescence, there is physical growth and change, and the sexual organs develop and begin to function.

During the last period of adolescence, many emotional changes take place, and problems may arise. The young person may feel adult in some ways, but still not want to act as an adult. New relationships with people will develop, and relationships with parents may be difficult. Adolescents begin to identify with groups of young people, or with some older person, or even form romantic attachments.

It is a period of so much change and development that the adolescent is constantly adjusting to new feelings in himself and in those he lives with.

WHY DO SOME FEMALES HAVE BIGGER BREASTS THAN OTHERS?

There is no such thing as a "normal" size for a woman's breasts. They vary in size, depending on a great many things, such as the general health of the woman, race, age, and even climate. So it is perfectly normal for one woman to have larger – or smaller – breasts than another woman.

There is an "average" breast size in a woman who has not had a baby, and that ranges from 4 to 6 inches in diameter.

IS IT WRONG TO HAVE SEX WITHOUT BEING MARRIED?

When we try to decide whether it is "wrong" to do something, we have to consider many things. What do we believe? How will we feel about it afterwards? What might be the consequences of it?

The desire for sexual intercourse is a natural one, and when married people do it they are not only enjoying a physical experience – they are also expressing their love for each other.

To have sexual intercourse without feeling love for the other person in a way reduces it to just a physical experience, so it means less and has less beauty and meaning.

Also, if a person's religion, or upbringing, say that it is wrong to have sex without being married, then doing it may make a person feel guilty and "immoral".

If unmarried people have sex and produce a baby, then there can be many problems and difficulties for themselves and for the baby.

WHAT IS CIRCUMCISION?

The forward part of the penis is called the glans. It is covered by a fold of skin called the "prepuce", or foreskin. In some cases, the foreskin may cover the entire glans. This may block off urine. It may also cause irritation and infection to take place there.

Removing the foreskin is called "circumcision". It is a simple operation and consists of cutting away the extra foreskin so that the glans is free. It is usually done a short time after birth.

Circumcision has been performed among certain people – such as the Jews – as a religious rite for thousands of years. Today it is done among most people for reasons of hygiene.

DO ANIMALS ENJOY SEX?

Yes. And that is the only reason they do it. They have an instinct that leads them to want to mate and have intercourse. They do not do it – as humans do – out of love, or the desire to have a child.

In many animals there is a period – which could be once or twice a year – when they are "on heat", or ready to mate. Among such animals, sex never takes place at any other time.

WHY DON'T PARENTS TELL THEIR CHILDREN ABOUT SEX?

It depends on the parents. Some parents still think of sex as something "nice children" should not know about. This attitude is considered old-fashioned and not right today.

Other parents want their children to learn about sexual intercourse, why it is done, how it is done, and what it can mean in a person's life. But they find it difficult to discuss such things with their own children, not because they are "ashamed" of it, but because it is a subject that is so personal, it can be embarrassing for them to talk about.

Your parents want you to know about and understand sexual attraction and intercourse. That is why they bought this book for you.

WHY IS SEX DONE IN PRIVATE?

Sex is a very intimate and personal experience. It is carried on by two people who want to express their love for each other this way. It is done in private out of a feeling of respect for this emotion and experience they share.

IS THERE A "NORMAL" SIZE FOR A PENIS?

No. Some males have a large penis, some have a smaller one. There is an "average" size among adult males, and that is about six inches long when it is erect.

WHAT IS A HOMOSEXUAL?

A homosexual is someone who wants to have any kind of sexual activity with a person of the same sex.

It is not "homosexual" if there is only great friendship and affection between people of the same sex. The desire for sexual activity is what makes a person a homosexual.

ARE THERE MALE AND FEMALE HOMOSEXUALS?

Yes. Though many young people usually think of homosexuals as being males, there are female homosexuals, too. They are called "lesbians". The name is derived from the island of Lesbos, where in ancient Greek times, a woman poet, Sappho, lived and wrote about women who loved each other.

HOW DO HOMOSEXUALS HAVE SEX ?

Male homosexuals handle each other's penis so that there will be an orgasm.

Female homosexuals caress each other's body, and stimulate each other's sex organs so that they will both experience an orgasm.

WHAT MAKES A PERSON A HOMOSEXUAL?

In every human being there are both male and female elements. Normally, feminine elements predominate in the female, and masculine elements predominate in the male. This has usually taken place by the end of puberty.

But some adolescents and pre-adolescents live through certain situations and emotional experiences that cause homosexual tendencies to develop. For example, there may be a fear of the opposite sex, or the boy may identify very closely with his mother, or a girl very closely with her father, and make it impossible for them to have intercourse with members of the opposite sex.

The reasons for a person becoming a homosexual are often so complicated, however, that there is still no scientific "rule" about why it happens. Experts believe that it is *not* a matter of being born homosexual or having a different kind of body structure.

DO HOMOSEXUALS WANT TO BE HOMOSEXUAL?

Nowadays, many individuals openly admit that they are homosexual, and are saying they are proud and happy to be so.

Many others, however, would rather not be classified as such. Some try to hide it, or try to get treatment to rid themselves of their tendencies.

But medical science, including psychiatric help, has still not found the complete answer of how to deal with and help such people, because it is a very complex problem.

WHY DO MANY PEOPLE MAKE FUN OF MALE HOMOSEXUALS?

In our society, people have developed the image of the ideal male as being very masculine and "manly", the opposite of the feminine, so they tend to belittle males who do not live up to that image. In a way, a male who takes the female role in a homosexual relationship is attacking their idea of how society should be, so these people resent it.

DOES A WIFE HAVE TO HAVE SEX WITH HER HUSBAND WHENEVER HE WANTS TO?

In a marriage, the wishes and needs of both the husband and wife should always be considered. People who love each other want to, and try to, act this way. But this does not mean a wife has to have sex with her husband when she does not want to, or when it would disturb her physically or emotionally to do it.

WHAT IS A PROSTITUTE?

Prostitutes are persons who will have sexual intercourse with anybody who will pay them money to do it.

WHAT ARE NOCTURNAL EMISSIONS?

"Nocturnal" means it happens at night, and an "emission" is something that is sent out, so a nocturnal emission is the discharge of semen from the penis that happens at night while the male is asleep.

It has happened to every male, and there is nothing "wrong" or harmful about it, and no reason to feel any shame or guilt about it whatsoever.

Why does it happen? There are millions upon millions of sperm cells in the male reproductive organs, and new ones are constantly being produced. The accumulation of semen in the "seminal vesicles" (the organs which store the semen) creates a physical pressure. It may result in an erection of the penis and then ejaculation of semen – an emission. And it can occur spontaneously, that is, without the male even knowing it is taking place. He will not know about it until he wakes up and finds his pyjamas are wet with this sticky substance.

It may also happen when the male has erotic dreams – dreams associated with sex. Because of the emission that takes place, they are sometimes called "wet dreams". It is a perfectly natural and normal thing for this to take place.

CAN A WOMAN HAVE SEX MORE OFTEN THAN A MAN?

Yes. After a male has an orgasm, his penis becomes soft, so he cannot have intercourse until he has another erection. This may take some time.

After a female has an orgasm, her vagina is still able to have intercourse, and so she can have sex again without waiting. For this reason, a female can have sex more often than a male.

HOW LONG DOES INTERCOURSE LAST?

There is no set time. The process of having intercourse may include preliminary steps, such as kissing and caressing each other, which can last as long as the two people wish.

The actual time the penis is in the vagina before there is an ejaculation also varies. The average time for younger people is about two to three minutes, and somewhat longer for older people.

WHAT IS THE FUNCTION OF THE PENIS?

There is a small tube that runs through the centre of the penis which has two functions. One function is to serve as a passageway for urine, which comes to it from the bladder. The other function is for sperm to pass through it during sexual intercourse. There are special valves which prevent urine being passed with the sperm cells during ejaculation. These valves also prevent sperm cells being passed with urine.

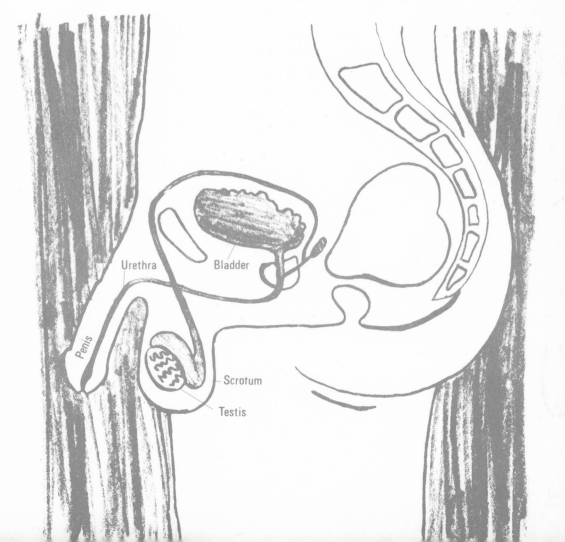

WHAT IS SPERM?

Sperm is the male sex cell. When it unites with an egg cell inside the female, a new life is started.

Sperm cells are developed in the male testes, which hang between the thighs in a pouch of skin called the scrotum.

When the male has an ejaculation during intercourse, the muscles of the penis contract and force sperm out of the penis and into the vagina. Millions of sperm cells are ejaculated at one time.

The sperm cells travel to the female egg cell. A sperm cell is about 1/500 of an inch long, with a head, a middle section or body, and a tail.

The sperm cell is able to move because of the lashing motions of the tail. The head of the sperm contains the genes – the material that carries the heredity from the father for the new child.

Only one sperm can enter the egg cell, and the first sperm cell to arrive is the one that does it.

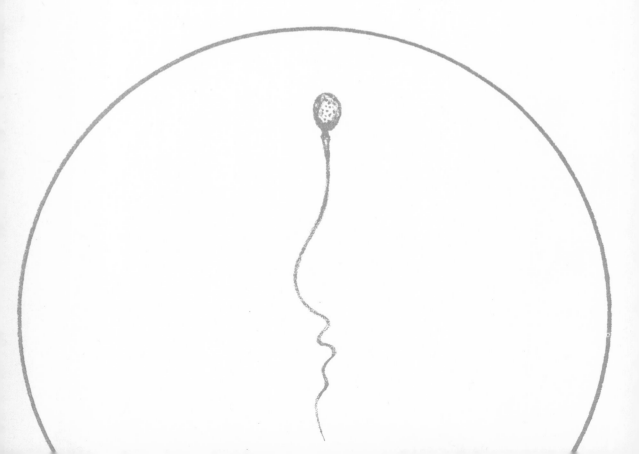

HOW LONG DO SPERM CELLS STAY ALIVE?

This is not known exactly, but it is believed that sperm cells stay alive in the vagina for up to 48 hours.

WHAT IS EJACULATION?

An ejaculation is the contraction of the muscles of the penis that force the sperm cells out. The fluid that comes out contains not just the sperm cells, but secretions from several sex glands.

During an ejaculation, the male feels stimulated not just in the area of the penis, but in other parts of the body, and even mentally.

WHAT IS "NECKING"?

Necking is a way of expressing affection. Boys and girls do it quite naturally to show how they feel about each other. It may just be holding hands, or putting an arm around the waist or neck, or kissing. It does not involve sexual intercourse.

WHAT IS "PETTING"?

Petting is the kind of lovemaking between a male and female that prepares them, or arouses them, to have sexual intercourse – even though they may stop and not have sex.

In petting, the sensitive parts of the body are touched and caressed, such as the breasts of the female, and each other's sex organs.

When a couple is about to have intercourse, they start showing their love and desire for each other by petting.

CAN PETTING PRODUCE AN ORGASM?

It depends on how far it is carried. If the male caresses the female's clitoris, she can have an orgasm. If the female caresses the male's penis, he can have an orgasm.

IS PETTING WRONG?

Petting is only wrong if it makes the people involved feel guilty afterwards. However, it must be realised that petting can lead to sexual intercourse because of the intense sexual desire it can arouse.

Petting can give the male and female great pleasure, and it enables them to express the way they feel about each other.

WHAT IS THE CLITORIS?

In a way, the clitoris is the female's "penis". It is a soft, buttonlike organ located at the top of the vagina, and is covered by a fold of skin.

It has very sensitive nerve endings. The clitoris can be compared to the penis because it also has erectile tissue. This means that when it is touched or stimulated, it becomes firm.

For the female, it is the organ that provides sexual pleasure during intercourse.

HOW DOES A FEMALE BECOME PHYSICALLY "READY" FOR INTERCOURSE?

In the male, it is simple: the penis becomes erect. In the female, it is more complicated. The vagina becomes moist as certain glands inside it send out secretions. It also expands as more blood flows into it. And the clitoris may become firm.

A female's whole body becomes ready for sex.

WHAT IS RAPE?

Rape is when a man forces a female to have sexual intercourse against her will.

How can he force her to do it? By struggling with her until she can no longer fight back, or by threatening her with a weapon, or by striking her.

DO THE MAN AND THE WOMAN HAVE AN ORGASM AT THE SAME TIME?

Sometimes it does happen, and it is considered desirable by some people. But in most cases it does not occur at exactly the same moment. This need not make any difference in the enjoyment of the intercourse.

DO SOME WOMEN NEVER HAVE AN ORGASM?

Most women do not have an orgasm during the first few times they have intercourse. And some women never have an orgasm. But they can still become pregnant, have children, and feel happy in their married life.

The reasons for some women not having orgasms may be physical – such as when the male does not proceed in a way that makes it possible for her. Or there may be mental or emotional reasons for it.

WHAT IS A DIAPHRAGM?

A diaphragm is one of the devices used to prevent conception – the fertilising of an egg by a sperm.

It is a rubber cap, about three inches in diameter. It is placed in the vagina, over the cervix, and closes off the entrance to the uterus. This keeps the sperm from entering. The diaphragm is placed in position by the woman before sexual intercourse.

A diaphragm can be obtained only by prescription from a doctor, and must be fitted by a doctor. It must be used with a special cream or jelly which kills sperm cells.

A diaphragm must be left in the vagina for eight hours after intercourse.

WHO IS RESPONSIBLE IF AN UNWANTED PREGNANCY OCCURS?

Both partners are equally responsible. The decision to have sexual intercourse is an adult one and both the man and the woman must make sure that precautions are taken to prevent pregnancy.

DO A HUSBAND AND WIFE HAVE INTERCOURSE, ONCE THE WIFE BECOMES PREGNANT?

The desire by the female to have intercourse does not disappear when she becomes pregnant. But there are certain times during her pregnancy when intercourse could be dangerous to the baby or to her own health. Her doctor will advise her about this. It varies with each individual.

Generally, it is believed by doctors that intercourse should be avoided during the first three months of pregnancy, and during the last six weeks. But for some women it is considered safe to have intercourse during the early months of a normal pregnancy.

HOW OFTEN DO BOYS AND MEN HAVE ERECTIONS?

Since an erection can be caused by a great variety of situations, there is no way of estimating its prevalence. For example, many males have an erection in the morning when they may have to urinate. An erection can be caused by certain thoughts, or by dreams, or by what one is listening to or reading, or by seeing an attractive female. So most males have frequent erections.

WHY DO ANIMALS HAVE INTERCOURSE?

The chief reason animals have intercourse is to reproduce. The animal does not know that this is the reason for mating – it merely follows an instinct nature has given it to carry on the species.

Among most animals, mating takes place only when the female is "on heat". This means that she has just ovulated – the eggs have descended and can be fertilised. During this time the female gives off a certain scent which attracts the male animal and arouses him sexually.

The female animal does not want to have intercourse at any other time than when she is on heat.

CAN A MALE BECOME SEXUALLY AROUSED WITHOUT WANTING TO BE?

Yes – and it happens to almost every male, because sexual feelings in him can be aroused quickly and for a variety of reasons. The male may often discover that it has happened almost without his knowing it.

AT WHAT AGE DO A GIRL'S BREASTS DEVELOP?

The exact age, and the exact way in which a girl's breasts begin to develop, depends on the individual. But the first changes in the female breast usually begin when she is between 11 and 13 years old.

The breasts become bigger, the nipple protrudes a bit more, and the area around the nipple (the "areola") has some colouring. The breasts at this time are usually cone-shaped.

Between 14 and 16, a layer of fat appears under the skin, which makes the breasts rounder.

DOES IT TAKE LONGER FOR A FEMALE TO BE SEXUALLY AROUSED THAN FOR A MALE?

Usually this is the case. A female feels the sexual impulse later in life than a male does. It usually takes longer for her sexual feelings to be aroused, and they are just as intense as the male's.

IF YOU DON'T HAVE SEX, WILL SOMETHING HAPPEN TO YOUR SEX ORGANS?

No. Sex organs are not like muscles that must be exercised to be able to be used. They do not grow weak because they are not used.

People who have no sex at all before they get married find that their enjoyment of sex is as great as anyone else's.

WHAT IS SYPHILIS?

Syphilis is a contagious disease acquired through sexual intercourse. It is one of the "venereal diseases" – diseases derived from sexual contact.

Syphilis is caused by a germ that penetrates the skin of the sex organ and enters the bloodstream and tissues.

About 10 to 90 days after the infection, a rash appears – on the penis, the vagina, or wherever the syphilis germ entered the skin. About 60 days after the infection took place, a sore, or "chancre", appears there. This disappears in 10 to 40 days – even if there is no treatment for the disease – but it does not mean the person no longer has syphilis.

Months later, or longer, the sores may appear again and do great harm to the body. The heart, the blood vessels, and the lungs may be affected by syphilis.

There is no way to prevent being infected by syphilis if one has sexual contact with a person who has the disease. The treatment for a person who has syphilis – or has had contact with someone who has the disease – is a series of penicillin injections. This treatment lasts about five days and is usually effective.

WHAT IS GONORRHOEA?

Gonorrhoea is a venereal disease – a contagious disease that is transmitted by sexual intercourse.

In the male, germs that cause it enter the opening of the penis and multiply in the tube (the urethra). The first symptom of gonorrhoea is an intense burning sensation when urinating. Later on, a large amount of pus appears, which may last for two to three months.

In the young female, a form of gonorrhoea can be acquired by contact with certain articles (such as towels) that were contaminated by someone with gonorrhoea. Her sex organs become infected and the infection may spread to the reproductive organs inside the body.

A person who has any reason to think he or she may be infected with gonorrhoea should see a doctor at once. Penicillin injections can clear it up quickly in almost all cases.

CAN A "VIRGIN" BECOME PREGNANT?

If a female has sexual intercourse, of course she can become pregnant, but if she does not have sexual intercourse, and her hymen is still intact – can she become pregnant? (The hymen is the layer of tissues which surrounds the outer opening of the vagina).

There is an opening in the hymen through which menstruation takes place, and so sperm can enter and make the female pregnant. It might possibly happen if a male's penis ejaculates near the hymen. But pregnancy in such cases is very rare.

WHAT IS ADULTERY?

When a married person has sexual intercourse with a partner outside the marriage, it is called adultery.

Adultery is considered to be grounds for divorce and it is condemned by most religions of the world.

Some societies accept what we call adultery or regard it as a private matter.

DO PEOPLE SOMETIMES HAVE SEXUAL INTERCOURSE WITHOUT PLANNING TO DO IT?

When two people are emotionally attracted to each other, they may show their affection by embracing and caressing each other. This can lead to the arousing of sexual desire and having intercourse – when they originally had no intention of doing it.

Later on, the couple may find it hard to believe that they could not stop, or understand why they could not. This is what makes sexual desire such a powerful force in life.

DO PEOPLE WANT TO HAVE SEX, EVEN THOUGH THEY ARE NOT IN LOVE?

Having sexual intercourse can be a beautiful part of being in love. But a person may still want and need to have sexual intercourse without being in love. It is a natural physical need. Of course, it cannot be the same kind of experience, as beautiful and important, as when it is done with a person one loves.

CAN A PENIS GET STUCK INSIDE A WOMAN'S VAGINA?

No. It is impossible and cannot ever happen. Anyone who says that it is possible does not know the truth, or is saying it to frighten someone.

WHY DO MEN SOMETIMES SEEK PROSTITUTES?

There are many reasons, and it depends on the individual. It can be because a man is not in love with anyone and feels a need for sexual intercourse. Or he may be away from home and feel this need.

In some cases, a man may even be married and in love with his wife, but the sexual intercourse they have may not satisfy him, and so he will go to a prostitute.

WHY ARE WORDS ABOUT SEX CONSIDERED "DIRTY"?

There are many people who regard any mention of sex, or use of certain words connected with sex, as "bad manners", "impolite", or "dirty". Of course, they have a right to feel like this, and a person should not offend them.

Other people, however, can accept a frank way of discussing sex, and even certain words – but not other words that are used. This is probably because they have been taught and brought up not to talk about sex in public, so it is hard for them to change their attitude.

Many adults feel it is wrong for children to discuss sex or to use certain words – but all right for adults to do so. This is probably the way they were brought up and trained, and they are doing what they think is best for their children.

Today, more and more young people are talking about sex very frankly, and using certain words without feeling they are "dirty". But it is always important to respect how other people feel about such things – whether they are strangers, friends, or one's family.

WHAT IS "SEX APPEAL"?

Males are attracted to females, and females to males – and "sex appeal" is a combination of the qualities that create this attraction. In a male, it may be a muscular body, a handsome face, or voice, or personality. In a female, it may be her figure, her breasts, her face, or eyes, or her smile. "Sex appeal" is a general term for whatever draws male and female together.

WHAT DOES IT MEAN WHEN A PERSON IS "FRIGID"?

Usually, this refers to females who are "cold" when it comes to responding to sexual intercourse. It does not mean the female cannot become pregnant and have children.

There are many different reasons for a female being "frigid", but they almost always have an emotional background. It may be because her early training made her feel sex was "nasty", or she may think that becoming pregnant would be a terrible experience.

Sometimes a female cannot respond sexually because of what the male does or does not do during intercourse – such as being clumsy, or ejaculating too quickly, or even some annoying personal habits he may have. Frequent quarrels and misunderstandings with the male can also lead to this lack of sexual response. This does not mean that she cannot respond under different circumstances.

CAN A FEMALE HAVE SEX WHILE SHE IS MENSTRUATING?

Yes. And in many females the desire to have sex is even heightened during the menstrual period.

But there are some religions that forbid intercourse during this time. Many people consider it "unclean" to do so, and others believe it is better for the female to "rest" during this period.

From the medical point of view, there is no physical harm in having intercourse during menstruation.

CAN YOU TELL BY LOOKING WHETHER A PERSON IS A HOMOSEXUAL?

No. Except, of course, if the person deliberately dresses or acts in a way intended to show the homosexuality. But in most cases a homosexual cannot be identified by appearance or behaviour.

ARE THERE MANY DIFFERENT POSITIONS FOR SEXUAL INTERCOURSE?

Yes. Many people believe there is only one "normal" position – the female lies on her back with the male above and facing her. But any position which satisfies both the male and the female, and does not offend either one, can really be considered "normal" for them.

Some of the other positions most often used are: the female lies on top of the male; they lie on their sides facing each other; the female lies on her stomach with the male over her; the female lies on her side with the male behind her.

CAN A MALE HAVE "TOO MUCH" SEX?

From the physical point of view – no. Having intercourse frequently, having many ejaculations, does not harm or weaken the male in any way.

DOES THE SIZE OF A MALE INDICATE THE SIZE OF HIS PENIS?

No. There is no relationship at all between the size of any other part of the body and the size of the male's penis.

WHAT IS PUBIC HAIR?

It is the hair that grows around the sex organs in both males and females. In males, it grows about the penis. In females, it grows in a triangular shape around the vagina. The colour of pubic hair is usually the same as the hair on the head.

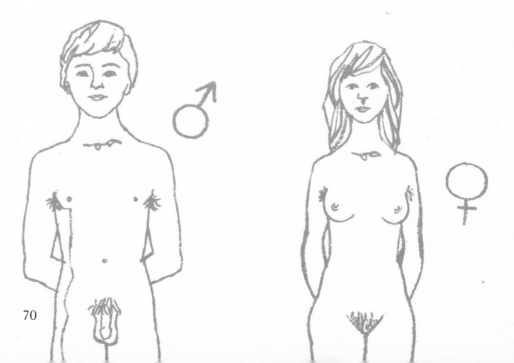

D-71

WHAT IS A PIMP?

A pimp is a man who gets customers for a prostitute and who controls her money and sometimes even how she lives. A pimp may have several prostitutes whom he "manages" in this way.

WHAT IS CASTRATION?

When the testicles of a male are cut off, we say he is "castrated". Since it is in the testicles that most of the male hormones are produced, the removal of the testicles prevents the development of some of the male characteristics – such as a beard or a deep voice.

In ancient times, conquering armies sometimes castrated enemy soldiers. In more recent times, in certain countries, young boys were castrated so they could serve as obedient servants or even as singers in choirs.

WHAT IS INCEST?

When sexual intercourse takes place between two people who are extremely closely related, for example a father and daughter, it is called incest. Incest has been forbidden by many societies because it is considered to be medically dangerous.

If children result from incest, they are likely to inherit the weakest characteristics, physically and mentally of both partners because of the way that certain types of genes from members of the same family tend to combine.

The laws on incest vary from country to country. In Britain it is a criminal offence for a male to have intercourse with his grand-daughter, his daughter, his sister and his mother. It is an offence for a female of or above the age of sixteen to consent to intercourse with her grand-father, her father, her brother or her son.

DO BOYS HAVE ORGASMS
BEFORE GIRLS DO?

Almost all boys do, because they start masturbating at an earlier age, and have nocturnal emissions ("wet dreams").

By the time they are 15 or 16, practically all boys have experienced orgasm. Most girls become sexually aroused at a later age. But by the age of 19 or 20, most girls have experienced orgasm either through sexual intercourse or masturbation.

WHAT HAPPENS WHEN A FEMALE
IS HAVING AN ORGASM?

A great many things happen at the same time, and in many parts of the body, because the female orgasm is a complex reaction.

The female has been sexually aroused up to this point, and now comes a heightening of excitement and a "release".

The heart beats faster, blood pressure rises, the walls of the vagina contract in a kind of rhythm (as do other muscles in the body), the clitoris is erect.

All of this is happening at the same time and the female does not feel each part of it separately – just an intense sensation of excitement and pleasure that comes to a climax.

When it is over, a kind of relaxation takes place in the sex organs and the whole body. It may take as much as half an hour before she feels all the effects of the orgasm are gone and she is "back to normal".

CAN FEMALES HAVE MORE THAN ONE ORGASM AT A TIME?

Yes. Some females want (and try) to have more than one orgasm at a time. Some females cannot do this. And some have multiple orgasms without even trying. Each of these kind of experiences can be considered "normal".

Usually, when females have more than one orgasm during the same sexual experience, it happens in a kind of "up-and-down" way. The excitement builds up, there is an orgasm, the intense excitement comes down, then builds up again. The time between each orgasm can be only a few seconds, a few minutes, or longer. And it can happen from twice to 20 or 30 times or more.

DO THE FEMALE BREASTS PLAY A PART IN SEX?

Yes. A female's breasts have two functions. One is to supply milk to the baby if she becomes pregnant.

But a female's breasts also give her pleasure when having sex. The nipples become hard, the breasts swell up, and she may enjoy having them caressed or kissed. The male also gets pleasure from doing this.

CAN A PENIS BE TOO SMALL FOR A VAGINA, OR A VAGINA TOO SMALL FOR A PENIS?

No. The vagina is one of the most elastic organs there is. During childbirth, it stretches so that a baby can pass through it. When it becomes moist during sexual excitement, if softens and is able to stretch so that any size penis can enter it.

CAN INTERCOURSE BE PAINFUL FOR THE FEMALE?

When a female has intercourse for the first time – or the first few times, in some cases – there may be slight pain or discomfort. But after that, there should be no pain at all. If there is pain during intercourse, it is a sign that something is wrong and a doctor should be consulted.

AT WHAT AGE DO MALES STOP HAVING SEX?

It depends on the individual. But in most cases, males stop having sex by the time they are 70.

CAN PEOPLE BE HAPPY WHO NEVER HAVE SEX?

Yes. Millions of people live happy and fulfilled lives without ever having sexual intercourse. But if the reason for not having sex is some emotional disturbance or problem, then such people can feel frustrated and unhappy.

Babies

Babies

HOW DOES A FEMALE GET PREGNANT?

Pregnancy begins when a sperm cell and egg cell unite. When the sperm cell fertilises the egg cell, it is called "conception", the start of a new life.

When a male has an ejaculation from his penis, semen – which contains millions of sperm cells – enters the vagina. The sperm cells go to the end of the vagina, to an opening called the cervix. They go into the uterus, or womb through this opening.

Female egg cells, produced in the ovaries, come down into the uterus through tubes called "Fallopian tubes".

The millions of sperm cells swim toward these tubes. If there is an egg cell there, the sperm cells surround it and try to get inside it, or penetrate it.

If one sperm manages to do this, the wall of the egg cell becomes hard so that no more sperm cells can enter. The sperm cell "fertilises" the egg cell, that is, it becomes part of the nucleus of the egg cell. This process is the conception of a baby. At that moment, the female is pregnant.

WHEN DOES THE LIFE
OF A BABY BEGIN?

A new life begins at the moment the sperm cell of the male fertilises the egg cell of the female. We say this because a new living thing is created at that moment, an egg-sperm cell that will become a baby.

WHY DOES IT USUALLY TAKE NINE
MONTHS BEFORE A BABY IS BORN?

In mammals, the period between the fertilising of an egg and the birth of the young that develops from that egg is called gestation. In human beings, the gestation period is about 280 days. It takes that long for all the changes and growth and development to take place so that the baby will be able to survive when it is born.

Among animals, the gestation period varies and is both longer and shorter than for human beings. For example: mice, 19 days; squirrels, 44 days; dogs, 63 days; horses, 336 days; elephants, 624 days.

IN WHAT PART OF A WOMAN'S BODY
IS THE BABY DEVELOPED?

Almost immediately after the egg is fertilised, the cell begins to grow. It does this by cell division – one cell becomes two cells, and so on. It is now called an "embryo", and it still remains in the tube where fertilisation took place, but it is moving towards the uterus, or womb.

Then it enters the uterus, and by the time the embryo is ten days old it begins to burrow its way into the walls of the uterus. Here is where it will grow and develop until it is ready to be born as a baby.

The uterus, a pear-shaped organ about the size of a fist, provides nourishment and protection for the developing child. As the baby grows, it stretches or expands. It can do this because the walls of the uterus are elastic, capable of being stretched to almost 500 times its original size!

The baby is protected inside the uterus by two coverings. The outside covering keeps it attached to the wall of the uterus. The inside covering is filled with a liquid in which the baby floats. The liquid is like a cushion that protects the baby from being bumped while the mother moves about.

The baby grows and develops here until it is ready to be born.

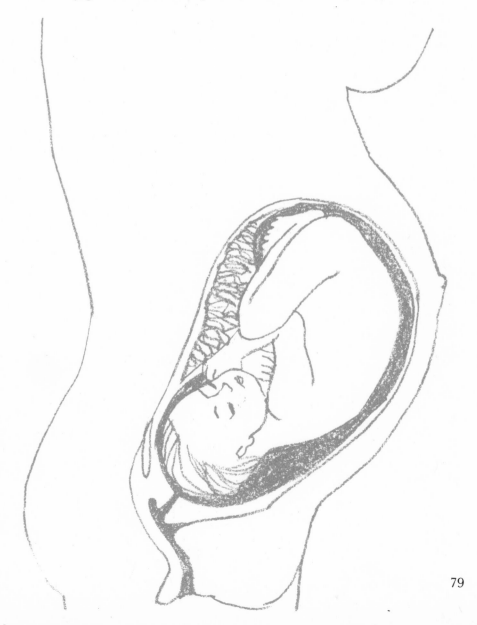

HOW DOES A BABY BREATHE INSIDE THE MOTHER'S BODY?

The baby receives oxygen – and nourishment – directly from the mother by means of a collection of blood vessels, called the "placenta", shaped like a flat cake. The placenta is connected to the embryo by a cord called the "umbilical cord".

Food, water, and oxygen from the mother's blood go into the blood vessels in this cord, and so into the baby. But the baby is already manufacturing its own blood, so the mother's blood does not go to the embryo.

WHAT EXACTLY HAPPENS IN THE PROCESS OF GIVING BIRTH TO A BABY?

The process is called "labour". It is the muscular contractions of the uterus which push the baby out into the world.

When the baby is ready to be born, the muscles of the uterus, or womb, start to contract. This is the first stage of labour. The muscles contract and relax, contract and relax. This may last from 9 to 14 hours.

This contraction breaks the two coverings that have surrounded the baby, and the water that has protected it flows out through the vagina.

Now the second stage of labour begins – the coming out of the baby. This may last from one to two hours, but with mothers who have already had children it may be a much shorter period.

In almost all cases (96 per cent), the top of the baby's head is the first part of the body to appear at the opening of the vagina. The vagina is spreading wide to allow the head and the baby to emerge. But since the head is so large, this is usually the most difficult and painful part of childbirth. The bones in the baby's head move closer together and overlap slightly to make the head a little smaller at this stage, so it will not be damaged.

The doctor holds the head gently to help guide the baby out. The contractions of the uterus continue, and the head of the baby is pushed out still more.

The mother helps the birth proceed by "bearing down". She does this by straining the muscles in her diaphragm, back, and stomach every time the womb contracts. Because this is such a necessary part of helping the birth of the baby in most cases, the mother is not "put to sleep" by the doctor. But certain gases and drugs may be given to make the mother's pains less intense.

After the head of the baby comes out completely, there is a short period when the contractions stop. Then they resume and the rest of the baby's body comes out. This part takes only a short time, compared to the time it took for the head to emerge. Now the second stage of labour has ended.

In the third stage, which happens in just a few minutes, the uterus contracts a little more and the placenta comes out, together with the two coverings that protected the baby inside. This is called the "afterbirth".

Then the doctor ties and cuts the umbilical cord, which connected the mother and child. The "belly button" we all have is the scar that shows where the umbilical cord was attached to us.

The baby starts to breathe – and the process of childbirth is over.

WHAT IS "NATURAL CHILDBIRTH"?

Some mothers would rather not have any anaesthetics during childbirth. They want to have the experience of feeling everything that takes place and doing all they can themselves to help the baby to be born. This is called "natural childbirth".

The mother, with proper ante-natal care, can learn special breathing techniques and exercises which relax her and enable her to have her child without the use of anaesthetics.

WHEN DOES A BABY'S HEART BEGIN TO BEAT?

The heart of a baby is formed by the joining of two blood vessels underneath the head. This tube grows quickly, bends around itself, and forms the structure that becomes the heart.

The heart begins to beat during the third week of the baby's life.

EMBRYO AT THREE WEEKS
(ACTUAL SIZE)

WHY ARE THERE SOMETIMES TWINS OR TRIPLETS INSTEAD OF ONE BABY?

Twins occur once in every 88 births. Triplets once in about 7,700 births.

There are two types of twins, fraternal and identical. This is what happens to produce fraternal twins. A female has two ovaries where eggs are produced. Occasionally one ovary releases two eggs at once, or each ovary releases an egg at the same time.

This means that there could be two eggs in one Fallopian tube, or an egg in each tube. Since these tubes are where sperm cells fertilise eggs, both eggs could become fertilised when sperm cells appear there.

If two eggs have been fertilised, each will become an embryo in the uterus, and will be born at the same time.

Fraternal twins may be of the same or opposite sex, and will only resemble each other as brothers and sisters do.

Identical twins are produced when a fertilised egg, after it is in the uterus, divides itself into two parts. Each part becomes an embryo, and both embryos develop and then are born at the same time.

Identical twins are of the same sex and look alike, which is why they are called "identical".

WHAT IS A FOETUS?

During the nine months the baby is in the mother's womb, it grows and develops.

At first it is called an embryo. An embryo is about an inch long at the end of six or seven weeks. In three months it is about four inches long.

At four months the embryo is six inches long, has arms and legs that can move, and is beginning to develop bones.

In general, however, the embryo is called a foetus after about the first two months of development.

WHAT DETERMINES THE SEX OF THE CHILD?

When a sperm cell fertilises an egg cell, the baby that is created inherits characteristics from both parents. But whether the child will be a boy or a girl is decided only by the sperm cell.

This is because all egg cells are alike when it comes to deciding the sex of a baby. But there are two kinds of sperm cells. One kind contains the X chromosome, the other kind contains the Y chromosome. The X chromosome produce girls, the Y chromosome produces boys.

So, depending on which kind of sperm cell fertilises the egg, it will be a boy or a girl.

By the way, it is not possible to know until the baby is born whether it is a girl or a boy.

AT WHAT AGE CAN A GIRL HAVE A BABY?

Being able to produce a baby means having egg cells that can be fertilised by sperm cells. This begins to take place when a girl starts to ovulate, which is at the age of puberty. Her ovaries start to produce ripe egg cells about once a month, and the egg cells enter the Fallopian tubes, where they can become fertilised.

This can happen in some cases before a girl begins to menstruate, so a girl can become pregnant even before she menstruates. Ovulation usually starts when a girl is about 13 or 14 years old.

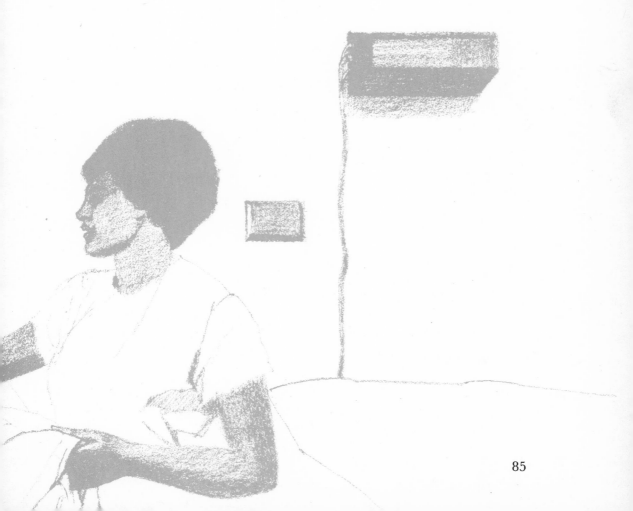

HOW SOON AFTER A COUPLE ARE MARRIED CAN THE WOMAN BECOME PREGNANT?

It depends on individual cases, but generally it takes more than two months. In some cases it may be eight or ten months before a newly married woman can become pregnant.

WHERE DOES THE MILK COME FROM TO NURSE THE BABY?

It is made in the mother's breasts. But in order for the milk to be produced, certain hormones have to start working in the breasts, and this happens when a woman becomes pregnant.

Actually, milk starts to be produced only after the baby is born. Human milk is a bluish-white or yellow colour and tastes sweet. It contains all the food elements the baby needs – carbohydrates, fats, and proteins. It also contains all the vitamins except B and D. And there are antibodies in this milk to help the baby fight infection.

WHY ARE SOME BABIES BORN LARGER THAN OTHERS?

When fertilisation takes place and a baby is created, that new baby is a mixture of what it inherited from the father and mother.

Exactly what it inherits is decided by little bodies called "chromosomes" which are in the sperm and egg cells. Chromosomes mix in a certain way so that the new baby will inherit a particular colour of hair, eyes, shape of nose, everything it is – including size of the body. The size of the baby is not decided by what or how much the pregnant mother eats.

87

WHAT IS ABORTION?

An abortion is when the foetus is deliberately removed from the uterus before it is 12 weeks old – so that a baby will not be born.

It is a simple surgical operation and it can be safe if it is done by a doctor in a hospital. It can be dangerous if it is done by a non-medical, unskilled person.

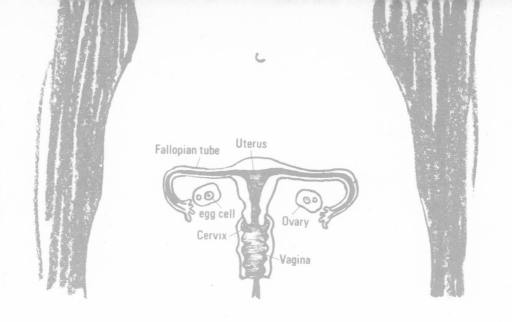

Fallopian tube Uterus

egg cell

Cervix

Ovary

Vagina

WHAT ARE THE FUNCTIONS OF THE OVARIES?

The ovaries are two organs in the female body, one on each side of the womb, where the egg cells (ova) are developed and stored.

Each ovary is about the size of an almond. The ovaries also produce several hormones that regulate the female reproductive system.

WHAT IS MENSTRUATION?

Every month, an egg in one of the ovaries becomes mature. That is, it is ready to be fertilised.

The egg leaves the ovary, enters the Fallopian tube, and moves towards the uterus. The uterus – just in case that egg will become fertilised – becomes lined with tiny blood vessels and cells that would help nourish the egg.

But if the egg has not been fertilised, the blood and cell layers are not needed, so they are sent out of the body through the vagina. This is called menstruation, and it lasts for about three to six days.

Menstruation is not "bleeding", even though there is some blood (only one to three ounces) in the fluid. Menstruation is a normal discarding of some tissues that the body does not need.

WHEN DOES A GIRL BEGIN
TO MENSTRUATE?

There is no exact timetable – it varies with the individual girl – but generally a girl begins to menstruate between the ages of 11 and 14. About 80 per cent of all girls have menstruated by the time they are 14. Yet some do not do it until they are 18. So a girl can be "early" or "late" and be perfectly normal.

IS MENSTRUATION PAINFUL?

Menstruation can produce both physical and emotional reactions in a female.

Since certain changes in hormones are taking place, it can have an effect on the emotions, make the female depressed, irritable, or moody. Physically, it can produce headaches, or abdominal pains. All this usually ends in a day or two.

WHAT IS THE MENOPAUSE?

This is sometimes called "change of life". It takes place in women usually between the ages of 45 and 55, and it may last from six months to three years.

During this period, the ovaries stop producing an egg cell every month, so menstruation also slows up and then stops altogether.

When the menopause period begins for a woman, she may have symptoms like hot flushes, headaches, dizziness, nervousness, loss of appetite. Some women become depressed at this time.

But after a while, the woman who has had "change of life" continues to enjoy life as she did before, including sexual intercourse.

DOES CONCEPTION TAKE PLACE EVERY TIME THERE IS INTERCOURSE?

No. For conception to take place, there has to be an egg cell in the Fallopian tube, and a sperm cell has to enter the uterus. Since an egg cell is not always there, and since sperm cells sometimes do not enter the uterus, conception does not always take place.

IF A GIRL "MISSES HER PERIOD", DOES THAT MEAN SHE IS PREGNANT?

If it is not just a delayed period, but is actually the stopping of menstruation, this is usually a sign of pregnancy. That is because a fertilised egg has attached itself to the lining of the uterus. The lining and blood vessels there are needed to nourish the egg, so they will not be discarded – that is, they will not be sent out through the vagina. There will be no more menstruation until after the birth of the baby.

WHAT IS AN EMBRYO?

An embryo is a fertilised egg cell. It becomes an embryo the moment it is fertilised, because it begins to grow at once – from one cell to many cells.

"Embryo" is the term used for an unborn baby from the time of conception to the ninth or tenth week. At this time, vital organs are already formed and the unborn baby is called a "foetus".

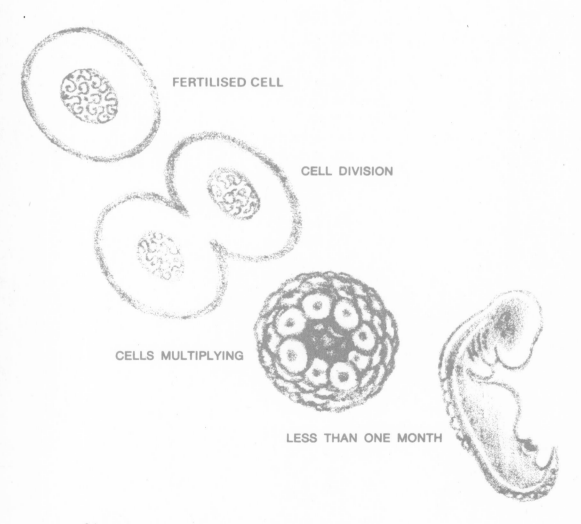

FERTILISED CELL

CELL DIVISION

CELLS MULTIPLYING

LESS THAN ONE MONTH

IS IT TRUE THAT A HUMAN EMBRYO HAS A TAIL?

In the very first stages of life, embryos of all higher animals look so much alike that they cannot be told apart. Even in the third week of development, the embryo of a human being resembles that of a reptile, a bird, or another mammal.

So, during the first month, the human embryo does have a tail – which later disappears.

HOW BIG IS THE EMBRYO AT THE END OF ONE MONTH?

Here are the sizes of the embryo during its development. One month: about a quarter of an inch long. Two months: about one inch long. Three months: about four inches long. Four months: six inches long. It is usually termed a "foetus" after about the two-month period.

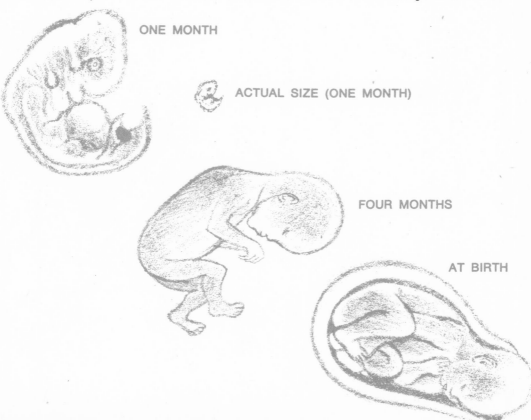

ONE MONTH

ACTUAL SIZE (ONE MONTH)

FOUR MONTHS

AT BIRTH

WHEN DOES THE MOTHER FIRST FEEL THE BABY MOVING?

Usually when it is about four months old, because by this time the bones have developed to the point where the arms and legs can move. The mother might say that she feels the baby "kicking", but it is a very gentle sensation.

WHEN DOES THE FOETUS BEGIN TO LOOK LIKE A HUMAN BEING?

It is hard to say exactly when this happens. But after eight weeks, when the embryo becomes a foetus, it definitely begins to look like an unborn human baby.

During the third month, the face changes a great deal. The eyes are in place, there is a bulging forehead, there are small, slit-like ears. There are nostrils, and a large, slit-like mouth. The upper limbs show the fingers, wrist, and forearms. By the end of the third month, the feet have toes, and the nails have begun to grow. There is no mistaking that it is a human baby now.

WHAT IS A PREMATURE BABY?

It is a baby who is born before it has reached full growth and development in the mother's womb. If it is less than 37 weeks old, it is considered a premature baby.

Babies that are born within 36 or 37 weeks after they were conceived are fairly well developed and have very good chances for survival. But babies born within 28 weeks after conception require constant medical supervision in order to survive.

Such a baby weighs about two pounds, its arms, legs, and hands are not developed, and its skin is wrinkled. This baby cannot be fed in the normal way or maintain a constant body temperature.

Hospitals have incubators, containers for such babies, in which proper temperature, humidity, and air pressure can be maintained.

A premature baby that has been given proper medical care begins to catch up in growth and development with normally born babies by the time it is two to three years old.

HOW DOES THE MOTHER KNOW WHEN THE BABY IS ABOUT TO BE BORN?

The baby will be born as the result of contractions of the uterus. The muscles of the uterus will squeeze tight, then relax, then squeeze tight, and so on. In this way it will push the baby out.

When these contractions begin, it is a sign that the baby is about to be born. The contractions feel like cramp, and are called "labour pains".

If the baby is actually on the way, the first few labour pains will be slight and about 15 to 30 minutes apart. Then gradually, the pains become more intense, last longer, and happen more frequently.

When a woman feels this taking place, she knows the baby is about to be born and goes to the hospital.

In some cases, there is another sign: a small amount of water may pass out of the vagina, caused by the breaking of the water-filled sac in which the baby was lying during pregnancy.

HOW LONG DOES IT TAKE FOR A
BABY TO BE BORN?

If a mother is having her first child, the period of labour (the muscular contractions that push out the baby) is generally 12 to 18 hours. For the second child and all other children, it is usually six to ten hours.

101

DOES IT HURT TO GIVE BIRTH TO A BABY?

Yes, there is a certain amount of pain involved. But there are several things about labour pains that make them quite different.

They are not continuous. The muscles of the uterus contract (painful), and then relax (no pain). The time between contractions gives the mother a chance to rest.

Also, these are "natural" pains. That is, it is not like having an arm broken or some kind of accident. The contractions of these muscles are a natural action of the body. The mother feels differently about these pains, since they are going to produce her baby.

Finally, the mother is given medicine that reduces the pain.

WHY DO DOCTORS USE FORCEPS WHEN A BABY IS BORN?

A doctor will use forceps only when necessary. Sometimes the contractions of the uterus, and the mother's efforts to help by "bearing down" on the back muscles, are not enough to force the head of the baby out.

Then the doctor uses forceps, which are special clamps, and applies them to the head of the baby. With the forceps he is able to move the baby's head and guide it out.

There is no danger to the baby because the doctor uses only a gentle motion of the wrist and the baby's head cannot be hurt.

WHAT IS THE FIRST THING A NEWBORN BABY DOES?

The newborn baby now has to start breathing on his own. To start his breathing, he utters a cry.

If the baby has not done this immediately after being born, the doctor will stroke its back, or slap it on the buttocks. This makes the baby cry and starts it breathing.

102

WHY DO NEW BABIES CRY SO MUCH?

A new baby cries because it may be uncomfortable, or it may be hungry. As it gets older, it can hold more food in its stomach at each feeding – so it does not cry as often out of hunger.

Sometimes babies cry because it is a form of exercise for them. They may not want or need anything – and still do a lot of crying.

DO BABIES HAVE TO LEARN
HOW TO SUCK MILK?

Babies are born with a sucking instinct, and they have strong sucking muscles to help them do it, so they do not have to learn how to suck.

But nursing includes swallowing the milk the baby sucks in, and a baby has to learn how to swallow during its first few feedings.

A baby is not fed from its mother's breast until about 24 hours after it is born. At first the baby does not get milk from the breast, but a liquid called "colostrum". It is watery and yellowish, and contains food plus certain substances that help protect the baby from infections. Then, about three to five days after the birth of the baby, the mother's milk appears in her breasts.

WHY DO MOTHERS NURSE THEIR BABIES?

Milk from the mother's breast is considered to be especially good for the new baby because it contains the food the baby needs. It also may contain substances which protect the baby from disease.

Other reasons for nursing a baby are that the milk is there when the baby needs it, the milk cannot spoil, and it is economical.

It is also believed that the baby gets a good feeding from being close to its mother all this time.

WHY DON'T ALL MOTHERS NURSE THEIR BABIES?

Some mothers simply do not want to do it, which does not mean they feel any less love for their babies.

Some mothers cannot do it. Their breasts do not produce enough milk, or produce it only for a short while.

If the mother's physical condition is not good, or if she has some disease, such as tuberculosis, her doctor will order her not to nurse the baby.

107

HOW MUCH MILK DOES THE MOTHER PRODUCE FOR THE BABY?

It varies with each mother, but on the average, a mother produces about three ounces of milk at each feeding during the first few days of nursing. By the end of the first week, it is about four ounces or more. By the end of the second week, she may produce five ounces or more at each feeding.

WHY DO MARRIED PEOPLE PRACTISE BIRTH CONTROL?

Birth control means using some method or device to prevent conception when intercourse takes place. In this way, married couples are able to plan their families. They decide when they are ready to have children, and how many they want to have. Then they use some birth-control method to avoid having more children than they can provide for and take care of, or having them too soon together. Birth control for married people is often called "planned parenthood".

There are many reasons why this is done. In some cases, it would be a hardship to have another baby – the cost of caring for it might be more than the couple can afford. Sometimes the wife's health is such that a baby – or another baby – would be too great a burden for her, or bad for her health.

There is also a feeling now, in most parts of the world, that population growth should be controlled. When there is overpopulation – more people on earth than the world's resources can take care of – then hunger, death, disease, war, all may result from it. So, today, some form of birth control is accepted everywhere.

IS THE CATHOLIC CHURCH OPPOSED TO BIRTH CONTROL?

No – if it is done in a "natural" way.

The Catholic Church believes that it is against the will of God to use "unnatural" methods of birth control, such as mechanical devices or medicines.

The "natural" way for a wife to avoid becoming pregnant is for her to have sexual intercourse only on certain days of the month. These are days before and after she menstruates, when there is no ovulation, so there are no eggs to be fertilised. This is called the "rhythm method" of birth control.

One of the problems that may arise with this method is that there is still no scientific way of knowing exactly when ovulation occurs for each woman. There are charts and instructions that are used for this purpose, but they may not work out exactly right in some cases.

WHAT IS A VASECTOMY?

Vasectomy is a simple operation that enables the male to continue to have sexual intercourse, but makes it impossible for him to make a female pregnant.

There is a tube that carries the sperm cells from the testicles to the penis, called the vas deferens. This tube is cut and the ends are tied. After this operation, called a vasectomy, there can be no sperm cells in the male's semen.

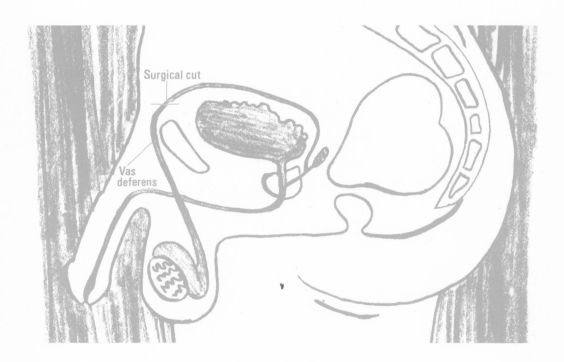

WHAT IS AN "ILLEGITIMATE" BABY?

An illegitimate baby is a baby born to a couple who are not married. It is called "illegitimate" – which means "contrary to the law" – because governments have established laws about marriage and families.

WHY CAN'T LITTLE GIRLS HAVE BABIES?

A female cannot have a baby until she has mature egg cells. These are egg cells, produced in the ovaries, which are released once a month. If such an egg cell is fertilised by a sperm cell, a baby is created.

But until a girl reaches a certain age (13, 14, or older), her body does not have such egg cells to be released – so a little girl cannot have a baby.

IS A BABY ALWAYS BORN HEAD FIRST?

Almost always. But sometimes the buttocks come out first, in which case it is called a "breech" delivery. Similarly, the face, or the shoulders, or the legs may come out first.

A doctor can often tell weeks ahead if something like this is going to happen. He then may be able to change the baby's position before it is born. He moves the baby around from outside the womb.

A baby that does not come out head first usually takes longer to be born.

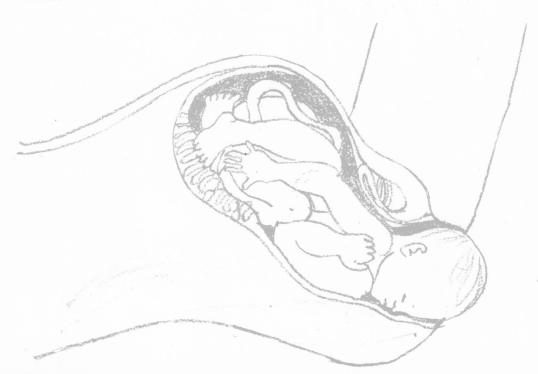

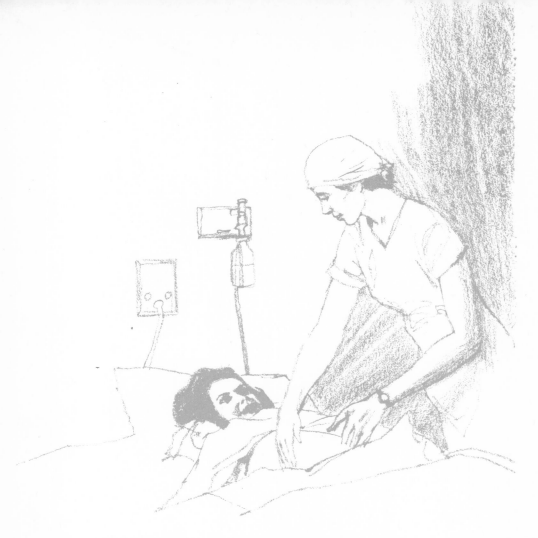

WHY DOES A WOMAN GO TO A HOSPITAL TO HAVE A BABY?

It is the safest thing to do because in a hospital there are doctors, trained nurses, technicians, and all kinds of equipment to take care of any emergency that may arise.

For example, if the baby cannot be born in the normal way, an operation may have to be done. Or the baby may need special care of some sort. And in a hospital, whatever can be done to help the mother before, during, and after childbirth, is done by trained people and with the best equipment.

WHAT IS A MISCARRIAGE?

When the foetus has developed for about 16 weeks and then leaves the mother's body before it can live as a baby, the expulsion is called a miscarriage.

There are many reasons it can happen, including the health of the mother, but in most cases it is because the egg was defective in some way and did not develop properly, so the uterus contracted and sent it out. It does not happen (as some people think) because the mother is shaken up physically or because she is emotionally upset.

A woman who has had a miscarriage can usually have normal pregnancies later on.

WHY DO CHILDREN RESEMBLE THEIR PARENTS?

In a child, certain things from both parents are mixed together. The male sperm cell and the female egg cell contain chromosomes. A chromosome is made up of genes – and the genes are the particles that transmit hereditary characteristics. This means that those things about a father and mother that can be passed on to a child are passed on through the genes.

This includes such characteristics as colour of skin, type of hair, shape of face, body structure, and other characteristics.

The way the genes mix – and the type of genes that come from the father and mother – decide what the new baby will be like. It may have hair like the mother's, a nose like the father's, and some features that do not resemble either one.

HOW DOES A FEMALE KNOW SHE IS GOING TO HAVE A BABY?

Certain signs and changes take place that usually indicate the female is pregnant. But they cannot be considered positive proof she is pregnant until she is examined by a doctor.

The signs, or symptoms, of pregnancy are:

She misses her menstrual period. But more than ten days must elapse since the period was supposed to have begun.

She has nausea (sometimes called "morning sickness"). She feels this about two weeks after the date of her missed menstrual period, and it lasts about six weeks.

There are changes in her breasts. They may become bigger, the nipples larger, and the area around the nipples become darker and wider.

She may need to urinate more often. This is because the uterus has become larger and is pressing on the bladder.

A female who has these signs or symptoms of pregnancy should see a doctor for an examination.

WHAT IS A "CAESAREAN" BIRTH?

This type of birth is named after Julius Caesar, who is said to have been born this way.

When the doctor decides for some reason – the baby may be too large, or it is in the wrong position, or the mother's physical condition requires it – he orders that it be a Caesarean birth, instead of a regular birth through the vagina.

The mother is put to sleep. The doctor makes an incision (cut) along the abdomen. The tissues of the abdomen are held aside or fastened back. Now the walls of the uterus are exposed. An incision is made in the uterus and the baby is ready to be delivered.

Using a pair of forceps or his hands, the doctor brings the baby's head into the right position, and the baby comes out of the uterus – it is born. The incision is then sewed up.

A Caesarean birth takes very little time, is painless to the mother, and has no effect on the baby's health.

WHAT IS STERILITY?

A person is sterile when he or she cannot produce offspring. Sterility can happen to both the male and the female.

A male may be able to have sexual intercourse, ejaculate, produce semen – and still be sterile. This is because there may be no sperm cells in his semen, or not enough of them, or they may not be active enough to fertilise the female egg cells.

A female may be sterile for many reasons. There may be some condition or disease of her reproductive organs. There may be some disturbance in her glands so that the eggs do not mature in her ovaries as they should, or the eggs may not be fertile. Or there may be something in the structure of her organs that makes it impossible for her to become pregnant. Sometimes it may even be due to a poor nutritional diet.

A doctor can determine what is responsible for a couple not being able to have children. In some cases he can advise or give treatment that will enable the female to become pregnant.

AT WHAT AGE CAN A BOY
MAKE A GIRL PREGNANT?

A male can make a female pregnant as soon as he can ejaculate, because this means he is producing semen with sperm cells that can fertilise egg cells. This usually happens when he is about 13 years old.

For the female to be able to become pregnant, she must be already ovulating, producing egg cells that can be fertilised. This usually happens about the time of her first menstruation.

CAN A FEMALE BECOME PREGNANT
WITHOUT HAVING INTERCOURSE?

Intercourse means placing the penis in the vagina and ejaculating there. Becoming pregnant means having an egg cell fertilised by a sperm cell. So the question is: Can a sperm cell reach the egg cell without the penis having been in the vagina?

The answer is that it can happen, though it is not usual. Sperm cells are very active and move with great power. If the male has ejaculated near the opening of the vagina, sperm cells may be able to enter the vagina, go into the uterus, and fertilise an egg cell there.

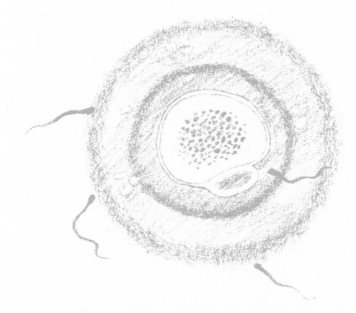

CAN A MOTHER INFLUENCE THE BABY INSIDE OF HER WHILE SHE IS PREGNANT?

No. No matter what happens to the mother emotionally or mentally – fright, shock, and so on – it has no effect on the baby.

There is no connection between the mother's brain and the child's brain. The only actual connection between the mother and the baby is the supplying of food and chemical substances to enable the child to develop and grow.

HOW OFTEN MUST INTERCOURSE TAKE PLACE TO PRODUCE A BABY?

There is no way of knowing the answer to this. There must be an egg in the Fallopian tube ready to be fertilised. There must be a sperm cell to reach this egg cell and fertilise it.

When this happens during intercourse, a baby is produced. When it does not, intercourse must take place to produce a baby. And it may not happen the next time, either – unless there is an egg cell in the right place and a sperm cell reaches it.

DOES IT HURT THE BABY TO BE BORN?

No. The largest part of the baby that has to pass through the vagina is the head. Before a baby is born, the bones of its head are actually separated, so that the head can be pressed together without doing it any harm.

After the baby is born, the open spaces are filled in by the growth of the bones in the skull.

CAN A NEW-BORN BABY FEEL ANYTHING?

At birth, a baby has everything he will need and use to feel, see, think, and experience sensations. But they are not all yet in a condition to be used.

For example, a newly born baby cannot focus his eyes, so things look blurred. But it can tell the difference between darkness and light.

The baby has taste sensations, feels the difference between hot and cold, and can feel pain. But it may take a day or two before he can hear sounds.

WHAT COLOUR WOULD A BABY BE IF ONE PARENT WAS BLACK AND ONE WAS WHITE?

If the black parent has no white ancestors, and the white parent has no black ancestors, their children would usually be an "in-between" colour.

If the two people have parents of different colours, their children may vary in skin colour from black (going back to the black ancestor) to white (the colour of the white grandparent or ancestor).

If one parent is light in skin colour, but has black ancestry, and marries a white person, the children will usually have skin colour no darker than that of the near-white person.

DOES WHAT THE MOTHER EATS AND DRINKS AFFECT THE UNBORN BABY?

If the mother has a normal, nourishing diet, the baby will grow and develop normally. If the mother consumes a great deal of alcohol, or smokes a great deal, or takes drugs – studies show that the child can be affected. How much and in what way depends on the individual case and what the mother takes in.

WHAT IS GIVEN THE MOTHER TO EASE THE PAIN OF CHILDBIRTH?

Basically, it is some form of anaesthesia – which dulls or eliminates any sensation. What kind of anaesthesia, and where it is applied, depends on the doctor and the condition of the mother.

A general anaesthesia – taken by inhaling gas – puts the mother to sleep so she can feel nothing. A caudal anaesthesia keeps the mother awake, but stops all sensation in the lower part of the body. A low spinal anaesthesia, given at the lower end of the spine, acts in the same way.

And an anaesthetic can be injected locally, near the vagina, so there will be no pain in that region.

CAN A FEMALE BECOME PREGNANT AT ANY TIME OF THE MONTH?

No. There is a time of the month for each female when conception is not possible. This is during the time she menstruates, and seven to nine days before, and three to five days after she menstruates.

The exact time when she cannot become pregnant depends on several things: her menstrual cycle (the number of days between menstruations), whether her cycle is regular (occurs after the same number of days each month), and how long she menstruates each time. It is not always possible to be precisely accurate about this.

WHY ARE BABIES "BURPED" AFTER FEEDING?

"Burping" a baby means holding it erect over the adult's shoulder and patting it gently on the back. It is done after each feeding and sometimes during the feeding.

Burping gives the contents of the baby's stomach a chance to settle towards the bottom. It also gives the air, which was swallowed with the milk, a chance to come up and be expelled.

HOW OFTEN IS A NEWBORN BABY FED?

Newborn infants require food about once every four hours. If the baby is smaller, it may have to be fed once every three hours. It depends on how long it takes for the baby's stomach to become empty — and this does not always happen on an exact schedule. During its first month, a baby usually has to be fed six or seven times a day.

HOW MANY HOURS DOES A NEWBORN BABY SLEEP?

A newborn baby sleeps 18 to 20 hours a day. Each period of sleep lasts from two to three hours, and then the baby is awakened by hunger.

As the baby grows older, and its stomach becomes larger, it can hold more food, so it can sleep longer each time.

When a baby is six months old, it sleeps less, about 16 to 18 hours a day, and it usually can sleep through the night without being fed.